KANDINSKY

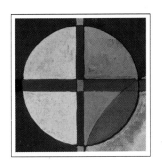

THE LIFE AND WORKS OF

KANDINSKY

Bekah O'Neill

A Compilation of Works from the
BRIDGEMAN ART LIBRARY

Kandinsky

This edition printed for :
Shooting Star Press Inc.
230 Fifth Avenue – Suite 1212
New York, NY 10001

Shooting Star Press books are available at special discounts for bulk purchases
for sales promotions, premiums, fund-raising, or educational use. Special
edition or book excerpts can also be created to specification. For details
contact: Special Sales Director, Shooting Star Press Inc.,
230 Fifth Avenue, Suite 1212, New York, NY10001

© 1995 Parragon Book Service Limited

ISBN 1-57335-123-7

Printed in Italy

Editors: Barbara Horn, Alexa Stace, Alison Stace, Tucker Slingsby Ltd and
Jennifer Warner.
Designers: Robert Mathias and Helen Mathias
Picture Research: Kathy Lockley

The publishers would like to thank Joanna Hartley at the Bridgeman Art
Library for her invaluable help.

Wassily Kandinsky 1866-1944

Often heralded as having painted the first abstract painting, Kandinsky sought throughout his work a new means of expression. Whether or not he did produce the first abstract painting, and there were many artists working towards the same goal at the same time, he was certainly one of the only ones to work towards 'non objective' painting with such a strong theoretical basis. Throughout his life he saw painting as connected with the other arts, and in particular with music. He associated colours with sounds, and wanted colour and form to exist purely for their own sake, as notes do.

Kandinsky came late to painting – he was already 30 when he began. He was born in Moscow in 1866 and had attended the university where he studied law and economics. After obtaining his degree he was offered a professorship but he declined, and instead worked for a while as a manager in a large printing firm, before he decided to embark on a career as an artist and so moved to Munich.

Munich at this time was a centre for art with the Munich Sezession and Jugendstil, the German version of art nouveau. When Kandinsky arrived with his wife Anya he enrolled in the private art school of Anton Azbé. Azbé taught in the traditional way, using models in life classes, but Kandinsky disliked these methods and stated that he felt 'more at home in the world of colour than the world of drawing'.

In 1901 Kandinsky founded Phalanx, a new association for artists to exhibit their work. There was also an associated art school where Kandinsky taught painting and life classes. It was here in 1902 that he met Gabrielle Münter, who was to become his companion until 1914.

After separating from his wife, he travelled widely with Gabrielle

Münter. They spent a year in Paris where Kandinsky published a series of woodcuts called *xylographies*. Up until this point Kandinsky's paintings had their roots in fairy-tale historical and romantic subjects and landscapes, very often painted with a palette knife. He had also experimented with a variety of techniques such as tempera, gouache and woodcuts. In 1908, after returning to Munich, he and Münter spent some time in Murnau, a small town beneath the Bavarian Alps. With fellow artists Marianne von Werefkin and Alexei von Jawlensky they spent the summer painting the views around Murnau. Kandinsky used this time to experiment with form and colour and to try and express the emotional as well as the representational. In this period we can see the gradual process of Kandinsky shedding the world of the representational and naturalistic, and working towards the abstract. Very often he would paint from nature, and then return to his studio to work from memory. This led to a use of heightened, intense, non-naturalistic colour which overwhelmed the subject. In 1909 Münter bought a house in Murnau and they spent every summer there until the outbreak of the First World War. Although at this time the subjects painted by Kandinsky were usually scenes from around Murnau, he still did not entirely dispense with the fairy-tale themes of his previous work.

In Murnau, Kandinsky and Münter started collecting glass paintings. Kandinsky experimented with this technique in both studies and finished works, the most famous being *All Saints*. In 1909 Kandinsky founded The New Association of Munich with Alexei von Jawlensky as vice president. They held the first exhibition in that year. In 1910 the second exhibition included an international collection of artists, including Braque, Picasso, Derain and Vlaminck. Kandinsky exhibited some of his own work in the exhibition, including *Composition 2*. Critics were harsh, and the exhibition provoked outrage.

In 1909, Kandinsky started painting works which he divided into three catagories: Impressions, which were inspired by nature; Improvisations, which were spontaneous reactions of his own 'inner nature'; and Compositions, which were the most involved, usually very large works, needing many preliminary sketches and studies. The choice of these titles shows Kandinsky's linking his painting to musical terms. In 1913 Kandinsky published a book of poetry illustrated with woodcuts called *Klänge* which literally means sound.

In 1911 Kandinsky, together with Franz Marc, formed the *Blaue Reiter* group, the Blue Rider Group. The first exhibition contained a wide variety of artists including Rousseau, Robert Delaunay and August Macke as well as composers such as Schönberg. The Blue Rider Group held two exhibitions and published an Almanac.

In 1912 Kandinsky published *Concerning the Spiritual in Art* which included chapters on 'The effect of colour' and 'The language of forms and colours' in which he investigated the expressive properties of colour and again examined the analogy between music and painting. Around this time Kandinsky had an experience in his studio, which helped him move further towards abstraction. He came home at twilight, to see 'an indescribably beautiful picture that was saturated with an inner glow'. He could see 'nothing but the shapes and colours and the content of which was incomprehensible to me'. He then discovered that this was one of his own paintings leaning on its side against a wall. Kandinsky tried to capture the impression that picture had given him, and realised that from then on the 'subject matter was detrimental to my paintings'.

At the outbreak of the First World War, Kandinsky was forced to return to Russia, where he lived until 1921. He held various posts as a Professor at Moscow University. In 1922 Walter Gropius offered him a Professorship at the Bauhaus in Weimar. The Bauhaus was closed in Weimar in 1925 and relocated in Dessau and Kandinsky worked there until it was closed by the Nazis in 1933.

In 1926 Kandinsky's second book *Point and Line to Plane* was published. Kandinsky relocated to Paris and was to stay there for the rest of his life. He continued to exhibit and work until his death in 1944.

▷ **The Blue Rider** 1903

Oil on canvas

RIDERS WERE TO BE a motif widely used by Kandinsky throughout his work, whether they were symbolic of the Horsemen of the Apocalypse, depicting Saint George or representing the ascension of Elijah to heaven in a Russian *troika*, a chariot driven by three horses, a symbol widely used in Kandinsky's later work. Riders were so often used by Kandinsky that he was able to reduce and simplify the outlines to the extent that they became hieroglyphs. However in this painting, which is one of the first depictions of a rider by Kandinsky in oil, the theme is romantic, evoking a kind of medieval chivalry, judging by the rider's costume. The treatment of the subject is lyrical, the horseman gallops across an open meadow in autumn with birch woods in the background. Kandinsky uses a technique of thickly applied spots and dashes of colour, similar to Monet.

▷ **Song of the Volga** 1906

Tempera on canvas

IN THIS PAINTING Kandinsky uses a theme capturing the spirit of Russian folk tales and legends. As so often in Kandinsky's work he does not literally illustrate a particular folk or fairy tale, but prefers instead to leave a certain amount of ambiguity. Around this time, 1902-7, Kandinsky was working on a series of poetic paintings like the one seen here, with lyrical subjects. There is an operatic feel to this work, as the title suggests and many of the figures appear to be singing. Kandinsky was familiar with operas, Wagner's in particular. Viking ships were a common motif used in *Jugendstil* art and the decorative elements in this painting show this influence as well. Kandinsky saw the difficulty of these 'coloured drawings' being viewed as purely decorative, with the subject being secondary, but it was his aim to not make the subject so clear and obvious that it could be instantly read. He wanted the content to be 'sensed', and he said of his work at this time 'the more one leaves to be guessed at and interpreted the better'.

◁ **The Looking Glass** 1907

Colour woodcut

THIS FULL COLOUR woodcut has a theme associated with romantic historicism with its roots in folk legend or myth. However this subject, which could have been treated purely decoratively, is endowed with association and meaning. Although the subject is not instantly recognizable as from a particular story, the figure holding the mirror obviously is doing so for a far deeper meaning than vanity. This woodcut has many Japanese elements: the treatment of the mountains in the background, the figure herself in her flowing robe and the rose-coloured cloud motifs. Kandinsky was familiar with Japanese woodcuts and this woodcut is printed on Japanese paper.

Houses in Munich 1908

Oil on cardboard

◁ *Previous page 13*

PAINTED WITH A LIGHT pastel palette, Kandinsky shows elements of life in Munich against the background of a street at sunset. Three figures are shown sitting in the centre of the foreground, two of them looking as if they are listening to the larger figure. The figures approaching this group look like they are carrying something. The posture of the walking figure on the far left is echoed by a black shadow of a figure walking in front of the tall yellow house. Strangely, this painting has an unfinished oil sketch on the reverse: this is unconnected to this painting and shows a landscape with a rainbow and figures.

▷ **Bavarian Landscape with Church** 1908

Oil on cardboard

IN THIS PAINTING we see Kandinsky using the glowing intense colours of the period spent in Murnau, particularly the blue and yellow combination used throughout his work. The church on the left is painted in solid, strong, flat areas of colour and outlined, which gives it the same qualities as a woodcut. This contrasts with the rest of the painting, where Kandinsky uses directional short brushstrokes, and where in some areas you can make out the background cardboard showing through.

△ **Landscape with Hills** c1908

Oil on cardboard

THIS PAINTING is very similar to *Upper Bavarian Mountains with Village* (see page 17) and seems to be painted from the same viewpoint. Characteristic of the Murnau period, Kandinsky has painted large areas of solid colour, in this case predominantly red, blue and green in the mountains and foreground, which contrast dramatically with the acid yellow and green of the sky. The solid areas of colour contrast with the dabs of colour in the sky and on the grass. The buildings are reduced to geometric shapes of solid colour, and the whole emphasis of the composition is on the horizontal.

△ **Upper Bavarian Mountains with Village** c1908

Oil on cardboard

COMPARED WITH *Landscape with Hills* (see page 16) Kandinsky uses a similar composition, but with the addition of some houses at the foot of the mountains and a tower, perhaps a church, which adds a vertical element to a strongly horizontal composition. The scale of the buildings, in comparison with *Landscape with Hills*, are, in this painting, more varied, less perfectly geometrical and have no black outline. The mood is far warmer than *Landscape with Hills*, there are more glowing red tones and less of an acid contrast between the sky and the mountains, which could be suggesting different times of day.

◁ **Railway near Murnau** 1909

Oil on cardboard

IN 1909 GABRIELLE MUNTER bought a house in Murnau and Kandinsky spent every summer there until the outbreak of the First World War. In his paintings of this period we see his technique develop away from the semi-impressionistic style of paintings such as *The Blue Rider* of 1903 (see page 9), and more towards an Expressionist style, using a palette similar to that of the Fauves. The palette used was predominantly red, yellow and blue and Kandinsky particularly used violent oppositions of the complementaries blue and yellow. In paintings of this period the influence of Bavarian glass-painting can also be seen, a technique that Kandinsky experimented with around this time and which is typified by strong hot glowing colours. The theme is unusual in Kandinsky's work as it is technological, although the subject of the train is almost toy-like and seems to develop out of the landscape.

◁ Murnau Landscape with Tree 1909

Oil on cardboard

KANDINSKY DEPICTS the familiar scenery of Murnau in this painting. The composition is unusual and the emphasis is strongly horizontal, with a band of dark blue above the green, which divides the painting almost exactly in half. This horizontal emphasis is broken by the vertical trunk of the tree in the foreground, which gives the painting deep perspective. Kandinsky uses strong contrasts of green and red in this painting giving it a rich quality. The brushstrokes are a mixture of tonal dabs, thickly overpainted, which contrast with the areas of flat colour seen on the roofs of the houses. In the large green area which occupies half the picture plane the brushstrokes are flurried and the background cardboard can be seen showing through.

△ The Road to Murnau 1909

Oil on cardboard

ALTHOUGH COMPOSITIONALLY this painting is similar to *Murnau with Rainbow* (see pages 22-23), the atmosphere created is much more dramatic. This is partly due to, the technique Kandinsky uses – directional diagonal brushstrokes, short stripes of colour combined with solid areas of luminous thick colour. The colours yellow, blue, green and red are dominant in this painting and are applied in such a way as to make the yellow road seem to tilt up and come towards the viewer, whereas the blue and green areas seem to recede. This effect combines to create a solid depth. The buildings are heavily and solidly formed. The three figures on the bottom left are unusual in Kandinsky's landscape paintings of the time: they seem to stare directly out and engage the viewer, and are placed in such a way as to lead the eye up the yellow road and into the painting.

▷ **Murnau with Rainbow** 1909

Oil on cardboard

THIS PAINTING is similar to *The Road to Murnau* (see page 21) of the same year in its distorted flattened perspective, although in this painting the picture field seems broken into two halves divided by the zig-zag of the yellow road, the dark half on the left contrasting strongly with the bright right-hand side. The two sides are bridged by the arc of the rainbow. In contrast to *The Road to Murnau* the brushstrokes used here are agitated, particularly on the left-hand side with the background of the cardboard showing through in some areas, or else these flurried brushstrokes are applied over solid areas of colour.

△ **Houses at Murnau** c1909

Oil on cardboard

AT THIS TIME Kandinsky often worked on a subject and then returned to the studio to let his imagination have a hand in his work. In this painting we see the same zig-zagging streets of Murnau as we have seen in *Murnau with Rainbow* and *The Road to Murnau* which were both painted around the same time. The houses are haphazard, and exaggerated, emphasizing the steepness of the hill, and they seem to topple over as they go up the hill towards the mountain. To avoid the houses becoming a patchwork pattern, Kandinsky uses a heavy black outline around them. The palette is dark and brooding and suggests night. In 1913 Kandinsky said 'for many years I have searched for a way of letting the viewer "go for a walk" in a painting and of making him lose himself in it'.

Women in Crinolines 1909

Oil on canvas

◁ *Previous page 25*

THIS LARGE CANVAS shows women dressed in typical *Biedermeier* fashion, a style prevalent in Germany and Austria in 1815-48. The subject goes back to the 1903-7 period when Kandinsky had used women in crinolines as a theme in woodcuts and paintings. In this painting he uses an almost classical frieze-like composition, the pediment of the building being directly in the middle of the canvas, creating a triangular shape with the figure in front echoing this shape. Kandinsky uses a predominantly green, yellow and pink pastel palette.

▷ **Improvisation 4** 1909

Oil on canvas

KANDINSKY USES the horse and rider theme again in this painting. We can see the brown horse moving left to right, with a cloaked rider and the horse turning its head back. It was from 1909 that Kandinsky started to divide his work into the catagories of Impressions, Improvisations and Compositions. The Impressions were direct in their naturalism and representation, the Improvisations were spontaneous expressions of his inner emotions and the Compositions were expressions of long-developed inner feelings which involved much preliminary work. In this Improvisation the mood seems dark and brooding, the rider is cloaked in black and Kandinsky uses a dark and heavy palette.

◁ **Improvisation 8** 1909

Oil on canvas

KANDINSKY gave this painting the additional title of *Tall Fellow with Sword* and it depicts a large standing figure with a huge sword standing at the foot of the city. The composition is an inverted triangle divided in two, with the sword placed directly in the centre of the painting, the city rests on top of the sword looking precariously placed and leaning inwards. Many of the brushstrokes are directed from left to right emphasizing the diagonal divisions of the painting. In sketches for this painting the figure to the left of the sword-carrying figure is equally prominent whereas in this finished version this figure blends into the background as do the female figures on the right. The theme is related to Kandinsky's earlier depictions of legends and court scenes and the figure could be interpreted as the Guardian of Paradise.

△ **Battle/Cossacks** 1910

Oil on canvas

Battle/Cossacks is often seen as a sketch for *Composition IV* (1911) although it seems highly finished for a sketch – it seems to be more a detailed treatment of elements to be used in *Composition IV*, dealing with what would become the left-hand section of the finished Composition. This goes along with Kandinsky's methods of working for his Compositions, which were his most fully worked out paintings, involving preliminary sketches and studies. Horsemen were often used by Kandinsky as a theme in this period, and here we see two battling horses with their hooves entwined forming horseshoe shapes. The riders both have red hats and yellow bodies, the one on the left with a green face, and they are fighting with pink sabres.

◁ **Murnau with Church II** 1910

Oil on cardboard

Murnau with Church II shows the village and the church of Murnau surrounded by the Bavarian Alps. Kandinsky worked through this subject many times: in a study for this painting the landscape is more recognizable and elements are given more of an outline and filled in with more solid colour. In *Murnau with Church II*, Kandinsky has obscured the landscape further by using feathery diagonal brushstokes, moving from right to left echoing the leaning of the church tower and the houses and mountains to the left. This creates a more dynamic, energetic feel to earlier versions and studies of the same subject. At this stage Kandinsky is still filling in colour within outlines, but using many patches of unrelated colour within these outlines, making images less instantly recognizable and so harder to read. When this work was shown at Kandinsky's first one-man show in Tannhauser it caused outrage among the critics.

Fragment of Composition 2 1910

Oil on cardboard

▷ *Overleaf page 32*

THIS OIL ON CARDBOARD deals with the right-hand side of *Composition 2* which along with *Compositions 1* and *3* were destroyed in the Second World War. As in his other compositions this was a large work involving many preliminary studies and sketches. The whole Composition dealt with the themes of destruction and salvation, the destructive elements on the left and in the fragment seen here the elements of paradise, which were dealt with on the right-hand side of the whole canvas. Kandinsky outlines the elements heavily in black and this combined with the light bright colours recall his paintings on glass.

▷ **Improvisation 11** 1910

Oil on canvas

ELEMENTS OF DESTRUCTION, chaos and deluge dominate this painting. On the right above the wheeled yellow cannon we can see a line of bearded featureless men, firing rifles with the smoke billowing out behind the dominant yellow triangle which could be the sail of the boat beneath it. Inside the wave-tossed boat is a red oarsman and three other dark figures. From behind the boat's sail there is another cannon, this one fires upwards, and above this are two men in red and yellow fighting with blue sabres. Above them on a brown hill shrouded hunched figures move across the painting to the left.

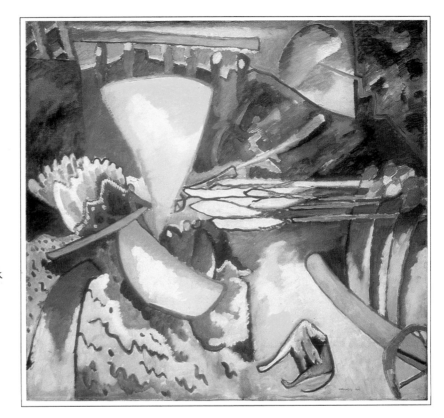

▷ **Improvisation 20** 1911

Oil on canvas

THE SUBTITLE OF *Two Horses* that Kandinsky gave this painting gives the motif away. Kandinsky's method of working towards abstraction was to include imagery that could be recognized, although these images would be hidden to some degree. By these methods Kandinsky hoped to avoid viewers finding his work inaccessible – after the initial recognition of the motif he hoped to then have engaged their attention so they could appreciate the 'inner resonance' of his work. The lines representing the horses and riders are placed directly on patches of colour which are not confined to these outlines, or contained within them, but spread and go beyond them. The partial depiction of horses and riders and the earthy colours used seem to resemble cave-painting.

◁ **Improvisation 19A** 1911

Oil on canvas

IN THIS PAINTING, Kandinsky uses colour in solid masses but uses thin outlines so the colours do not merge together and become totally unreadable. Although the motifs are elusive, what is created by this painting is a dark heavy atmosphere with the contrasting of lumpen shapes and hard dark lines. It seems to represent a landscape consisting of hills, mountains and figures. In the background we can make out the peaks of mountains and hills on the right; two finger-shaped forms, one red and one grey with a red upper part, seem to be leaning to the left and are moving up the hill; while below them an orange figure reaches out towards a dark figure below.

Lyrical 1911

Colour woodcut

▷ *Overleaf page 38*

THE TITLE KANDINSKY gave this woodcut links it to poetry and music. He had in fact done a version in oil earlier the same year, but he believed this version to be more successful – the subject seemed far more suited to the technique of woodcut where Kandinsky could use line in a more expressive way. The subject of horse and rider has been reduced and simplified to a few strong lines, no line is superfluous, yet within these few lines Kandinsky manages to express tremendous energy and speed. The few sparse lines representing trees on the left and on the right behind the horses lean inwards, and the surrounding colour of the landscape above and below echoes the shape of the horse, and add to the momentum by compressing down on the motif, emphasizing the sleek directional upward movement of the rider.

▷ **Landscape** 1911

Oil on canvas

KANDINSKY CALLED THIS painting *Romantic Landscape* – by this he means romantic in the sense of some kind of spiritual quest. The often-used theme of riders is seen again, in this instance three riders gallop down a mountain towards a brown tower which leans towards them, the tower is balanced by a dark solid form on the right, and it is these two leaning forms that seem to anchor the painting and prevent it from seeming too top-heavy. All the other emphasis in the painting is in the opposite direction. The technique Kandinsky uses of diagonal brushstrokes seems to emphasize the directional downhill movement and create a sense of dynamic immediacy.

▷ **Abstract Composition (Painting with a Circle)** 1911

Oil on canvas

KANDINSKY CALLED THIS the world's first abstract painting, although this is debatable as many artists in different parts of the world were individually and simultanuously working in an abstract style (for example, Mondrian and Delaunay in Paris and Malevitch in Moscow). Kandinsky was not happy with this painting at the time and did not include it in his private catalogue; it was only recently rediscovered in the store rooms of the Tblisi Museum in Moscow. It is hard to trace any motifs in this painting, which seems to consist of circles, circles being the most important of the primary forms in Kandinsky's work. It is a composition where all the emphasis is at the top of the painting, which is where the most distinct forms are, and as the eye works down these forms seem to dissolve and meld together. This reversal of gravity and its unusual composition give the painting a very heavy, solid feel.

Detail

▷ **All Saints** 1911

Painting on glass

THE THEME OF *All Saints* was depicted by Kandinsky in previous works. Glass painting was still being produced in Murnau in the traditional way which involved painting directly onto the reverse side of the glass. The glass paintings produced in Murnau were usually religious, and in this work Kandinsky chooses to represent the two Russian holy martyrs, Boris and Gleb, as the most dominant motif, as well as St Vladimir and St George along with other religious references.

◁ **Cover of Catalogue of**
Der Blaue Reiter 1912

Colour woodcut

IN 1911 KANDINSKY and Franz
Marc decided to form a group
and call it *Der Blaue Reiter*, The
Blue Rider. The name was
chosen as riders and horses
were often painted by both
artists. The image of the rider
was a dynamic one, a symbol
of quest and battle, ideal for
the launching of a new group.
 The woodcut shown here was
the cover of the *Blaue Reiter
Almanac* edited by Kandinsky
and Marc and shows a rider,
probably St George, as
Kandinsky had previously
painted a similar version of the
same subject but on glass. In
the glass version St George's
lance and shield and the
dragon are clearly visible, but
in this woodcut they are
obscured, possibly in order to
leave the figure ambiguous.

Legendary Animal 1912

Colour woodcut

▷ *Overleaf page 48*

THIS COLOURED WOODCUT,
which was worked on by Franz
Marc who founded the *Blaue
Reiter* along with Kandinsky,
was added to the deluxe
edition of the *Blaue Reiter
Almanac* in 1912. Kandinsky
stated that he wanted the
Almanac to 'establish links with
the past and project a ray of
light into the future'. The
Almanac was designed to be an
annual anthology of articles
and reviews with a
combination of original
illustrations, photographs,
examples of primitive art and
folk art and musical scores
contributed by composers like
Schöenberg. Paul Klee and
August Macke were just two of
the other artists included in
the group. The group held
two exhibitions in which artists
from all over the world were
shown including Rousseau and
Robert Delaunay, as well as
work from the Constructivists,
Cubists and Futurists. This
diversity of artists belonging to
the *Blaue Reiter* showed how,
unlike other groups, there was
no enforced style or
programme, the aim being
rather to examine the
theoretical problems of artists.

▷ **Improvisation 26** 1912

Oil on canvas

THE SUBTITLE OF THIS painting, *Rowing*, gives the motif away. Boats were a motif used by Kandinsky in scenes of the Apocalypse or Deluge. Unusually in this case, the boat is seen as the central image, a single motif being uncommon in Kandinsky's paintings. The figures in the boat are depicted in heavy outline as are the projecting oars. Kandinsky has liberated colour from the confines of outline – the colours lie side by side and overlapping with no defining borders, the outline of the boat filled with colour that overlaps and goes beyond it as well as being the same pink/red colour as the line of mountains behind. Kandinsky uses big areas of the complementaries blue and yellow: he believed yellow was a colour that appeared to come towards the viewer whereas blue seemed to recede. In this painting the overlapping areas of these colours creates a real feeling of depth and, added to the curve of the boat with the oars all tilting to the right, works to create an unbalanced rocking effect.

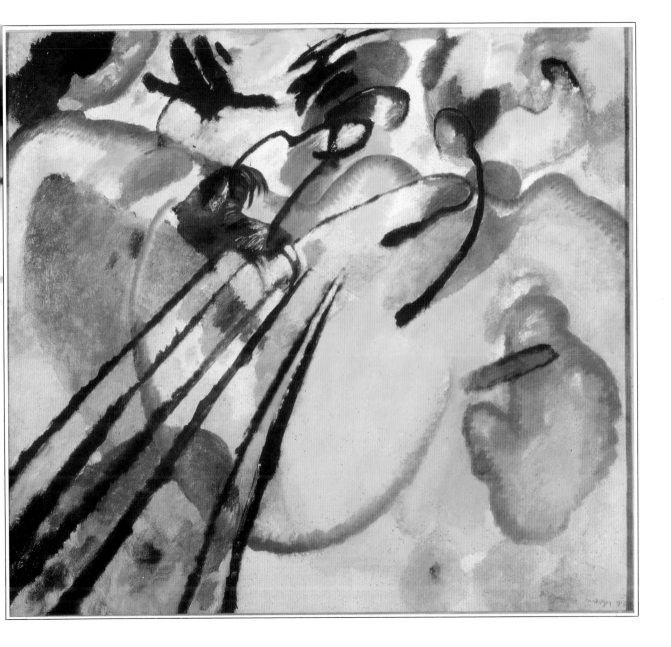

▷ **Improvisation 28** 1912 (Second Version)

Oil on canvas

IN THIS PAINTING Kandinsky further obscured motifs he had used in a previous watercolour. As in much of his work we see images of both destruction and harmony. In this painting the destructive elements are located on the left and images of hope on the right. On the left we see stormlike images, a wheeled cannon in the top left is placed in front of a mountain, below this are the four black lines of oars from a long brown boat. Dividing the painting are two transparent finger-like shapes, perhaps representing ghosts.

◁ **Landscape with Black Arch**
(and detail) 1912

Oil on canvas

THERE DO NOT SEEM to be any recognizable motifs in this painting. The composition consists of three masses of colour bound together by the black arch. Kandinsky uses the Russian word *duga* for the title, which could be translated as yoke as well as arch. Yoke seems more relevant as it appears to harness the three separate elements together. The top brown form is the most solid and geometrical, painted in almost solid colour with other forms inside it. Reading clockwise, the red form which bleeds off the bottom of the canvas is the largest of the three and the red colour which starts as solid at the top, seems to dissolve and fade to the colour of the background by the time it reaches the edge. The shapes contained within this form are less heavily modelled than the top shape and seem to float inside it. The third blue lumpen shape contains many echoes of the black arc, which can also be seen between the top and red forms. This echoing of the form suggests a rotation and despite the solidity of the forms the painting does not seem static.

△ **Sketch for Deluge 2** 1912

Oil on Canvas

ALTHOUGH THERE IS NO known final version of *Deluge 2* there is a similar sketch to this in watercolour. Kandinsky interpreted the theme of Deluge many times. Paintings on this theme contained elements from Noah's flood, stormy waves, lightning and subsiding boats. We can get the sense of this turbulence from this oil, even though we cannot make out specific images. The washes of colour combined with wispy black strokes create a turbulent chaotic mood. Kandinsky called the Deluge paintings *Sintflut* which translated from the German means the biblical flood rather than *flut* which is a flood of water, thus deliberately emphasizing the religious significance.

Small Pleasures 1913

Oil on canvas

◁ *Previous page 57*

WE ARE ABLE to identify many of the motifs in this painting from a painting on glass, on which this painting is based. The composition consists of a central panel and four corners. In the centre is a mountain with domed towers which have been reduced to geometric forms, above this is another mountain with its own towers, two riders gallop up the top mountain. The sun shines from the upper left and in the upper right we see a dark cloud. In the bottom right there is a rowing boat in a raging sea with three distinct black oars. Kandinsky wanted to 'Deluge the canvas with lots of small pleasures' which were walking, riding and boating. These 'pleasures' can also be seen as motifs frequently used in other works, such as the rowers in *Deluge* and the *Riders of the Apocalypse*.

▷ Moonlight 1907-13

Colour woodcut

In 1913 Kandinsky's poetry was published in a collection called *Klänge* , meaning sounds. This title related to Kandinsky's preoccupation with the relationship between music and art. He believed placing certain colours next to each other created certain effects like musical chords, and he wanted to show that art could convey its meaning through these combinations of colour, literally 'striking a chord'. *Klänge* consisted of 24 woodcuts, 12 in colour and 12 in black and white. In this woodcut Kandinsky uses a romantic theme with a *Jugendstil* influence,which was the German version of art nouveau, literally meaning 'the young style'. This influence is seen in the sinuous curving lines of the weeping tree, echoed in the hair of the figure beneath it. Although the influence of *Jugendstil* can be seen in Kandinsky's woodcuts it is not purely decorative but also emotional.

△ **Three Horsemen in Red, Blue and Black** 1907-13

Colour woodcut

THIS COLOUR WOODCUT was included in the first edition of *Klänge* and shows three horses and riders reduced to the most basic outlines, overprinted with floating coloured circles. Compositionally this woodcut reads from the centre outwards. Two horses seem to break out from the central blue coloured circle, one can be seen facing left and one right, both in profile with their rearing forelegs shown. The backs of the riders are indicated by a single line. The third rider heads towards the top border, he is much smaller and the whole horse is shown. The hard edges of the woodcut have been softened by the overprinted circles, the various flower and tree shapes and the way in which the two left-hand corners have been rounded off.

▷ **The First Abstract Watercolour** 1910-13

Watercolour, indian ink and pencil

THERE IS SOME DEBATE as to when this was painted: the most likely explanation is that it is an early study for *Composition 7* of 1913, as it contains similar motifs, seen especially in the central green and blue roughly circular forms within each other, with a rectangular outline cutting through them. This motif is common to all the sketches and studies for *Composition 7*. The arrangement is roughly circular and full of free-floating forms. It is anchored at the top right from which point the forms flow round towards the left, and the bottom two corners are rounded with two protruding lines on the bottom left, perhaps relating to the oars in the finished Composition. The light colours are complemented by the vigorous free black pen lines which add to the sweeping turbulent movement.

◁ **Apocalypse Riders** 1914

Painting on glass

THIS PAINTING ON GLASS shows
three of the four Horsemen of
the Apocalypse, a scene from
the Revelation to St John.
Kandinsky does not include
death, who is depicted as a
skeleton. We can identify the
three riders as horsemen of
the Apocalypse as the top rider
carries scales, the middle rider
carries a bow and arrow, seen
pointing downwards, and the
horseman on the lowest horse
has a sword pointing up. They
are shown leaping above a
small city on a hill, on which
sits St John of Pathos. This
glass painting is based on a
watercolour of the same date,
which does not include the
four animals seen in this
version which could be
representations of paradise,
the peacock being a symbol of
Eden.

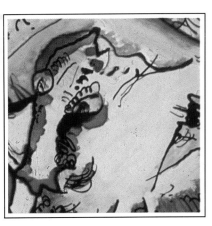

Detail

Composition 7 1913

Oil on canvas

▷ *Overleaf page 64*

DESPITE THE SEEMING spontaneous and arbitrary look of this painting, like all Kandinsky's Compositions it involved many preliminary sketches and studies, and in this case many different techniques – over 30 drawings, glass paintings, watercolours, woodcuts and oils. It is often viewed as Kandinsky's major work of the Munich period. The theme is catastrophy, containing motifs referring to both the creation and the end of the world. We can decipher some of these motifs from his preliminary work, although in this final painting the motifs are veiled, dissolved and abstracted further than they appear in the studies. The most distinct motif is a boat, a semi-circular shape, with three parallel black oars. Harder to decipher is an angel playing a trumpet, as if in the Last Judgement.

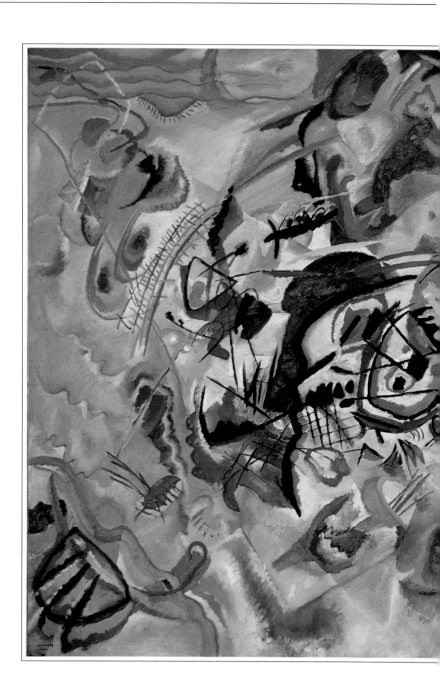

◁ **Two Ovals** 1919

Oil on canvas

KANDINSKY PAINTED a series of works to which he gave the title *Ovals*, these included *Grey Oval* in 1917, *White Oval* in 1919, the same year as this painting, and *Red Oval* in 1920. The composition consists of oval shapes floating in the centre of the canvas: the left-hand edge of the painting has been rounded off to emphasize the rounded forms. It is difficult to make out any recognizable motifs in this patchwork of decorative images, but there does seem to be a fish-like shape on the bottom right, and the sinuous lines and watery blues give the painting an underwater feel.

▷ **White Zig-Zags** 1922

Oil on canvas

THIS WAS KANDINSKY'S first
painting in Weimar, where he
had accepted a professorship
teaching at the Bauhaus.
An exercise Kandinsky
developed for his teaching
at the Bauhaus was a
questionnaire to show the
affinity between colour and
form. This is an exercise still
used today in many art
schools. The student was
given a picture of three
geometric shapes and asked
to fill in each with the
appropriate primary colour:
the results were that a very
large proportion of students
filled in the square red, the
triangle yellow and the circle
blue. This confirmed
Kandinsky's earlier theories
set out in *Concerning the
Spiritual in Art*.

▷ **Green Composition** 1923

Oil on canvas

THIS PAINTING IS also known as *Open Green*. Kandinsky referred to the paintings produced during his time in Weimar as cold and restrained. This painting is solidly constructed, with a strong diagonal emphasis. The corners are cut off, three diagonally, and in the top left by dissolving a red/pink circle. A mixture of pastel colours and a variety of textures are used, many of them seemingly transparent, with other forms showing through, a technique that adds depth. These transparent areas contrast with large areas of pure solid flat colour. We also see the black arc making a reappearance, this time looking similar to the accents in sheet music which increase or slow down movement.

◁ **Diagonal** 1923

Oil on canvas

OFTEN KANDINSKY would work on a neutral pale or white background in order to give his forms greater emphasis, and to project them forward. Many of the works painted in 1923-4 were constructed of diagonal lines. This painting has a strong diagonal movement from left to right shown by the main converging lines and culminating in the large lightning-like zig-zag at the top right. The emphasis is dynamic, but diffused somewhat by the motifs situated in the four corners and the intersecting forms. Kandinsky believed a movement from left to right was less dynamic than a right to left movement as the eye reads from left to right, and a movement in this direction is more expected and so less 'adventurous', as Kandinsky described it.

▷ **Hornform** 1924

Oil on canvas

THIS PAINTING HAS a grainy
rough texture, and the black
background is used as a base
for colours to dissolve into. We
see this around the yellow
hornform where the black
background takes on a yellow
tinge. This is seen also in a
purple tint dissolving around
the two pink perpendicular
lines. Rather than floating
freely, the elements are
anchored at both sides as well
as connecting and interacting
with each other. In some forms
where they connect and
overlay other forms, they
acquire a transparency seen
where the yellow *hornform*
connects with the grey form at
the bottom of the canvas, and
in other areas where two forms
overlap. The colours are pastel
and light; set against the black
background they acquire a
nocturnal, dream-like quality.

◁ **Swinging** 1925

Oil on board

Swinging WAS PAINTED in the same year that the Bauhaus moved from Weimar to Dessau. The title suggests a jazz influence with the variety of geometric forms arranged to create different rhythms. Jazz was a part of life at the Bauhaus where they had their own jazz band. The background of *Swinging* consists of neutral muted blues and greys which gives the tower-like construction of geometric forms greater prominence. Kandinsky's use of a combination of colours dissolving into one another, creating soft areas, contrast with areas of flat colour, and his use of black outline around the forms project them forward. As in other works of around the same time we see Kandinsky's use of the transparency technique, where one form overlays another and takes on another colour. Although *Swing* consists of many different intersecting geometric forms of differing sizes, the painting is solidly constructed and quite balanced compositionally.

Counterweights 1926

Oil on cardboard

◁ *Previous page 73*

Counterweights, or *Counterbalance*, as Kandinsky also called this painting, was painted in the same year as *Point and Line to Plane* was published in Munich. In this work Kandinsky examined the elements of form, point and line and their relationship to the plane, how different lines placed on the picture plane can have different effects on the viewer. He wanted to achieve 'through pedantic investigation of each separate phenomenon – both in isolation and interaction with other phenomena – to draw comparisons and general conclusions.' This composition consists of many circles, which to Kandinsky were the most important of the geometric forms used in his work. From the three primary forms, the triangle, square and circle, he believed the circle to be the closest to the 'fourth dimension'. He believed in the circles's 'inner force' and said that at this time in his work the circle was his favourite motif, in the same way that the horse and rider had been earlier.

▷ Square 1927

Oil on canvas

IN THIS PAINTING, which is similar to the work of Mondrian, Kandinsky uses the picture plane to suggest infinite space by placing a square within a square within a square, which could carry on indefinitely beyond the boundaries of the frame. This painting is based on an earlier watercolour of 1925 which is almost identical, apart from an intersecting black triangle breaking into the coloured chequers at the top, which Kandinsky does not include in the oil painting shown here. The colours used are predominantly monochrome and the colours in the patchwork chequers of the second square are muted, with the red and green squares most prominent.

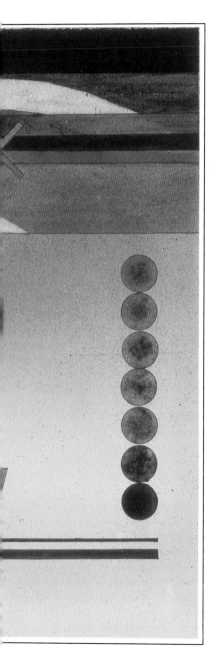

◁ **Pressure from Above** 1928

Watercolour

ALSO KNOWN AS *Pleasure from Above*, this watercolour illustrates some of Kandinsky's theories set out in *Point and Line to Plane*. In this book he said that according to where the forms in the picture lay, depending on their relationship to the edges of the picture plane itself, the nearer to the edges they were, the more tension the painting expressed. In this watercolour the forms are securely anchored at the top of the picture, the frame emphasized with thick bands of colour running right across the top edge and the other forms suspended from it, as if the border was compressing down on them. Kandinsky also said in *Point and Line to Plane* that forms lying near the borders of a picture would increase the 'dramatic' nature of the composition. This top-heavy suspended composition is emphasized by the dissolving and fading out of the red as we reach the bottom.

△ **Composition 10** 1939

Oil on canvas

Composition 10 was the last of Kandinsky's Compositions, and his last large canvas before the outbreak of the Second World War. It is unusual in that it is the only one of his Compositions to be painted on a black background. The many elements float freely within the painting, none of them anchored to any edge. The composition has an upward movement with the floating balloon-like elements. The hieroglyphs used on the brown circular shape are similar to those of Paul Klee, whom Kandinsky had known since 1912, when he had asked him to exhibit in the second Blue Rider exhibition and had published a drawing by Klee in the *Blue Rider Almanac*. They were both professors at the Bauhaus and shared many of the same views and theories on art and the 'spiritual'.

ACKNOWLEDGEMENTS

The Publisher would like to thank the following for their kind permission to reproduce the paintings in this book:

Bridgeman Art Library, London /**Stadt Museum, Mulheim,** Cover, Half-title, 73 /**Sammlung Buhrle, Zurich:** 9; /**Musee National d'Art Modern, Paris**/Lauros-Giraudon: 10-11; /**Kupferstichkabinett, Berlin:** 12; /**Heydt Museum, Wuppertal:** 13, 14-15; /**Christie's, London:** 16, 17, 48-49, 56; /**Stadtische Galerie im Lenbachhaus, Munich:** 18-19, 22-23, 36, 38-41 46, 51, 58-60; /**Kunstmuseum, Dusseldorf:** 20; /**Private Collection:** 21, 32, 69, 76-77; /**Mayor Gallery, London:** 24; /**Tretyakov Gallery, Moscow:** 25, 33, 35, 64-65; /**Collection Dr Ernst Schneider, Dusseldorf:** 27; /**Herbert Rothschild Collection, New York:** 28; /**Tate Gallery, London:** 29, 54-55; /**Stedelijk Museum, Eindhoven**/Lauros-Giraudon: 30; /**State Russian Museum, St Petersburg:** 43, 66; /**Solomon R. Guggenheim Museum, New York:** 52-53, 57; /**Musee National, Monaco:** 62-63; /**Museo d'Arte Moderno di Ca Pesaro:** 67; /**Pelikan-Kunstsammlung, Hannover:** 70; /**Nationalgalerie, Berlin:** 71; /**Galerie Maeght, Paris:** 75; **Stadtische Galerie im Lenbachhaus, Munich:** 44-45 **Musee National d'Art Moderne, Paris:** 61 **Kunstsammlung Nordrhein-Westfalen, Dusseldorf:** 78 **Tate Gallery, London:** 72